MODERN PUBLISHING'S EDITION

NEW KIDS

ON THE BLOCK

Handbook

an unauthorized biography
by Anne M. Raso

Modern Publishing
A Division of Unisystems, Inc.
New York, New York 10022

Book Design by Bob Feldgus

Printed in the U.S.A.

Table of Contents

The Kids must be worn out from thinking about their new Coca-Cola commercials, Saturday morning cartoon show, upcoming feature film, and "Magic Summer" concert tour.
Todd Kaplan, Star File Photo

Introduction

So, you haven't been able to get enough of the New Kids — those five adorable boys from Beantown who have taken the pop world by storm? Well, this "handbook," containing an astrological guide to the Kids, their proudest (and most embarrassing!) moments, intimate quotes, party picks, trivia and gossip — and lots more, has been written just for you! You are the ones who made the New Kids happen!

The Kids have been riding high on the charts for over a year now with their *Hangin' Tough* LP. And the release of their Christmas album, *Merry, Merry Christmas*, and latest LP, *Step By Step*, have only added fuel to the fire. Every show the Kids play is sold out, and judging from crowd reactions, as well as record, home video and merchandise sales, the New Kids are here to stay.

In the next year, look forward to seeing the Kids in five Coke Classic commercials, a Coca-Cola sponsored summer concert tour, their own ABC-TV Saturday morning cartoon show, and a feature film. There will be a new album from the movie soundtrack and a New Kids toy line from Hasbro is already on the shelves. Whew! No wonder these guys are called the "hardest working kids in show business."

New Kids Astrological Guide

How do you match up astrologically to your favorite New Kid? Are you their dream love match or their polar opposite in terms of personality traits? That's a very good question. And we're here to answer it!

Donnie Wahlberg
Birthdate: August 17, 1969
Birth Sign: Leo

Leos are big-hearted, very serious, and very intense about relationships. While most guys Donnie's age like to "play the field," Donnie usually gives 100 percent to one special lady, and he stays friends even after they stop dating.

To be Donnie's girl, you've got to have an assertive personality — the type who says hello to everyone, even people you don't know. You must be reliable — someone who will rush to a friend's side at the drop of a hat, and able to put other people's needs ahead of your own, just like Donnie does. Donnie likes girls from big families (just like his!) but it's not mandatory.

Donnie's potential date-mate must be smart and funny and able to deal with his forceful personality. She also has to be hip to the latest trends and understand why Donnie likes so many unusual fashion styles — including unlaced hightops and peace sign necklaces. (Oh, and don't make fun of those funny haircuts he sometimes gets — he's really open-minded when it comes to styles and is quite a trendsetter!)

Since Leo is a fire sign, Donnie is compatible with girls born under fire signs: Leo, Aries, and Sagittarius.

But that doesn't mean all the rest of you gals are ruled out. He says there are qualities he appreciates in girls born under every sign.

Donnie's favorite topic, other than music, is how to achieve world peace. He frequently wears a peace symbol and his favorite expression is "Peace out." *Steve Granitz/Retna Ltd.*

Danny's thick black hair is a dream for his hairdresser, Reynaldo Laureiro of Astor Place Haircutters in New York City. *Robin Platzer*

Danny Wood
Birthdate: May 14, 1970
Birth Sign: Taurus

Taureans are known to be stubborn, and Danny is no exception — he says that his stubbornness is probably his worst quality. People born under this sign are also practical and earthy, so it comes as no surprise that Danny likes girls who possess these traits.

Danny's ideal date-mate is someone warm and loving who will help him accept himself more (Danny can be quite self-critical at times). The *opposite* of a perfectionist would be perfect for this guy — a girl who can "live and let live." Danny likes a girl who is ready to hang out at a moment's notice and doesn't pay attention to dating "rules." Danny likes to see a girl when he's completely relaxed (not when there's touring, recording and other "heavy" topics on his mind). Darlin' Danny needs someone understanding who can tolerate his many moods and give him the emotional support he needs. No one fickle need apply for the role of Danny's girl — he needs someone very stable, like that number one lady in his life, his mom, Betty Wood!

The best match-ups for Danny are gals born under earth signs, which include Taurus (natch!), Capricorn and Virgo. What's the main thing Danny is looking for in a girl? SINCERITY, plain and simple. Girls who want to go out with Danny because he's a star can be counted out of the game immediately. Good luck getting this cool dude — he's never short on creative ideas for dates, though lavish dinners and other extravagances aren't his thing.

Joe McIntyre

Birthdate: December 31, 1972
Birth Sign: Capricorn

Capricorns are strong traditionalists and are the most conservative sign in the zodiac. So it comes as no surprise that Joe dreams of the day he'll marry that special girl and start a family as large as the one he grew up in. A Capricorn like Joe will woo you in the most romantic way — he'll send you roses, come to the door and meet your parents before a date (making sure to tell them when he'll get you home!), and hold open doors. You'll feel so special, you'll wonder how you ever went out with anyone else!

Joe's dream girl is someone who's funny and caring, and knows what to do when he's down (which, fortunately, is not very often). Joe wants someone with plain and simple tastes whose morals and ideals reflect a stable family life. He also wants someone who will appreciate that his idea of a romantic date is cruising in his car listening to the best of Frank Sinatra! (And don't be surprised if he takes you to Boston's Faneuil Hall Market and buys you a little memento — like a piece of hand-blown glass!)

Joe is really a traditional guy who only lives a "gypsy" life due to the line of work he's in. Being a fire sign, Joe is most compatible with those born under his sign, Virgos and Taureans. This guy will be loyal to you 'til the day you die!

Joe's idea of a romantic evening is to drive his date around Boston while listening to the best of Frank Sinatra.
Barry Talesnick/Retna Ltd.

Because of Jon's elegant look and interest in shopping for clothes, the other Kids call him "GQ." *Larry Busacca/Retna Ltd.*

Jon Knight

Birthdate: November 29, 1968

Birth Sign: Sagittarius

This Sagittarian loves to travel, and any potential date-mate of Jon's must be able to accept long separations, and be super supportive of his career.

What qualities do you need to hit it off with the oldest Kid? Well, you have to be mature because Jon is the Kid who keeps the rest of the group in line. He really appreciates a girl who possesses leadership qualities, does well in school, and is disciplined. At the same time, Jon's ideal date-mate must like to laugh, especially at the little things that go wrong in everyday life. Jon doesn't like girls who dwell on problems, but rather, those who look on the bright side of things.

Jon wants a girl who really understands what he does, but is not starstruck. He appreciates feedback on his work — but it must be HONEST! Jon expects a girl to have her own hobbies and interests and not to center her life around being a pop star's girlfriend. Jon admits that it's very hard to tell who's sincere and who's just latching on to him because he's famous.

Whatever your sign, you've got to have a zest for living to keep up with a guy like Jon!

Jordan Knight

Birthdate: May 17, 1970
Birth Sign: Taurus

Yep, there are two Taureans in NKOTB, meaning that some of you gals born under the right sign have a chance with *two* of these way-cool dudes! Jordan is fully committed to his work, and any girl who is a prospective date-mate should know this. But that doesn't mean he would ignore you when he's out on the road — no way!

What kind of girl is compatible with the younger Knight brother? How about someone who is fun-loving and sincere? If you have a reputation for being the life of the party, then this dude is for you. Like you, he has fun in all that he does and is almost always happy. Jordan is always the first person to send flowers to a friend who's sick in the hospital or who calls a sibling on their birthday. "Kindness" could be his middle name.

Jordan is also very spiritual and likes girls who put their faith in a higher power.

Fellow Taureans, Capricorns and Virgos are most compatible with this "Knight in shining armor," and he's most certain to be a dedicated date-mate. A holiday or birthday will always be spent with you providing he's not out on the road — and if he is, Jordan will remember to send an unforgettable gift.

Jordan bites his nails, snacks on candy bars, has never dated anyone steadily, and still doesn't believe that he is cute! *Chris Mackie*

Though Joe still loves to go bowling, golf is his latest passion.
Steve Granitz/Retna Ltd.

"Give Us A Break!"

Favorite Pastimes And
Behind-The-Scenes Activities

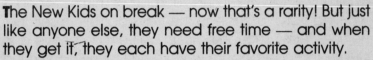

The New Kids on break — now that's a rarity! But just like anyone else, they need free time — and when they get it, they each have their favorite activity.

Donnie makes his hotel room into a home away from home. He always has plenty of bottled water, apple juice, and milk stored in his hotel room mini-bar. In addition, he has his free weights (packed up in a special case) and a CD player with a couple of dozen CD's to listen to while he works out. When there's time, Danny and Jordan come over to talk about projects for The Crickets (Donnie, Jordan and Danny's production/engineering/songwriting team that contributes a couple of cuts on each New Kids album). Donnie also uses some of his free time to daydream. He often thinks about what it would be like to stop all the wars in the world, and what he could do to make the world a better place to live.

Donnie also advises other young groups, and during the current concert tour, he's talking to a lot of music biz people, including on-air personalities, about two groups he's producing: his old friends, The Northside Boys, and his brother's group, Marky Mark and The Funky Bunch. Donnie hopes to have them signed to a recording deal by the end of the year, and has personally helped them pick out material for their demo tapes.

Donnie also plays drums, and pounding the skins is not only something he enjoys doing live onstage, but also just for fun.

Danny spends most of his free time on the road working out with weights although some of his favorite moments on the road are spent with his mom, who visits once a month. (Danny always says that his mom is his main reason for being successful today.) Danny loves to cook when he's got the time — and knows how to cook a roast or chicken to perfection.

Danny is always trying to improve himself, and is working hard to change the traits about himself that he likes least. Though he can be very defensive and stubborn, most people who know Danny don't mind because he has so many wonderful qualities.

Jordan's favorite pastime is to fool around on the keyboards during soundcheck. And he's really gotten good over the past year.

Jordan is very hard on himself and says he is the biggest worrier in the world. He still bites his nails though he's tried just about everything to stop — in-

What a rare sight! The New Kids relaxing. *Ebet Roberts*

It's not hard to believe that Danny spends most of his free time on the road working out with weights. *Ebet Roberts*

cluding painting them with that goop to make them taste really bad. But so far, nothing has helped. Jordan also twirls and pulls his hair, something his mother begs him to stop. (Mom also pushes him to get more sleep!)

Both on the road and at home in Boston, Jordan also likes to go shopping — something he frequently does with his brother, Jon. He also buys tons of magazines to read during flights and on the tour bus.

Jon is pretty easy-going and quiet, and is happy to spend leisure time at a mall or pizza parlor — providing he's got enough people around him to protect him. Shy Jon admits that he misses the days when he could walk on the street unnoticed! While at the mall, Jon usually can be found stocking up on Hostess chocolate cupcakes to stock away on the tour bus.

Jon also loves a good round of basketball with the guys and then taking his dog Houston for a walk. (Jon tends to lose track of time when he's out walking Houston so guess who's always the last Kid ready to go on?!)

Joe is studying both the piano and guitar, which you probably noticed if you caught any of the New Kids' winter concerts where adorable Joe dressed up as a guitar-playin' Santa. His current passion is golfing, although up until this point, he has failed to get any of the other Kids to join him. Joe also bowls a mean game, but says it's harder and harder to find bowling alleys on the road that aren't filled with kids who recognize him.

Joe is perhaps the most scholarly of the New Kids, and someday hopes to go to Boston College and major in journalism. In the meantime, he's keeping a journal of all the New Kids' road antics — something that's bound to become an untra-valuable tool for writing Joe's autobiography!

New Kids Style —
It's Sizzling!

The New Kids have such a "funky fresh" image that fans imitate their clothes, hairdos and mannerisms. Donnie describes their look as a combination of "street and slick." Since they've been together, their look has evolved and their management has given them more freedom to wear what they want onstage and in photographs. It wasn't so long ago that Maurice Starr, their producer, criticized the Kids for dressing like Run-D.M.C. and sent them back to the dressing room to change right before a performance.

Let's say you're a **Donnie** fan . . . What would you wear to emulate him? Well, the staples of Donnie's wardrobe are T-shirts with peace signs on them and ripped up jeans. (When the jeans are *too* ripped up, however, you can bet that someone from the group's management will have a wardrobe mistress talk Donnie into "tossing" them to avoid some embarrassing problems, such as patterned underwear hanging out of the holes!) Because they're so comfortable, white high-top Nikes are Donnie's preferred footwear. (Before the New Kids became famous, Donnie worked in a sneaker store, so he really knows his footwear and which sneakers can take the impact of an athletically-built dancin' machine!) Donnie also loves combining black and gold, and owns a lot of T-shirts in those colors.

Donnie's had a ponytail hair extension attached for over a year. The New Kid's hairdresser, the Argentina-born Reynaldo Laureiro of Astor Place Haircutters in New York, has done some wild 'dos for Donnie — the very wildest featured a peace sign shaved into

21

Donnie's very unique sense of style includes T-shirts, ripped jeans, peace signs, and high-top Nikes.
Larry Busacca/Retna Ltd.

the back of his head. Donnie experiments with a lot of different hairstyles, but usually has the top left about three times longer than the back. (The skinny ponytail attached in back gives the illusion of long hair.)

But what if you'd rather look like **Jordan?** Jordan balances the fine line between casual and dressy. He'll wear a suit jacket with jeans and sneakers — or to dress up such an outfit he'll wear a pair of suede slip-ons embroidered with gold emblems. Jordan wants all the latest styles as long as they're comfortable. Offstage, Jordan looks like the boy next door — except maybe for the gold hoop earring he wears in his left ear (all the boys have these except for ultra clean-cut Joe). Jordan wears his hair in a traditional pompadour cut, but has a very long skinny braid attached on back (an artificial hair extension), which has become his trademark.

Jon has an elegant, and yet conservative look (except for his earring). For his style and fashion sense, Jon has earned the nickname "GQ" from the other boys. He loves to shop when he has the time and it's not surprising for him to come home with six or seven pairs of dress shoes and Italian suits with padded shoulders. He prefers rugby shirts and jeans for casual wear, but tends to complete this look with fancy shoes (as opposed to sneakers). Sometimes he wears those preppy "docksider" shoes.

Danny's look is very hip. He wears ultra-baggy pants in dramatic colors such as red and yellow, and tops them with a tank top to show off his rippling muscles. (He usually removes his shirt during the show.) The bold colors Danny chooses look wonderful with his olive complexion and black hair. This flamboyant dude just has the best time trying new styles, but keeps comfort in mind when buying clothes.

23

Danny is equally experimental in his hairstyles — his only "constant" is the curly ponytail extension he has attached at the nape of his neck. His thick black hair is a dream for Reynaldo to work with, and late in '89 the Astor Place prized employee shaved a stripe right around the top of Danny's head.

Joe has the most simple style and the easiest to attain — he dresses just like any wholesome 17-year-old, except for the two large gold rings he wears on each hand for "street appeal." (The rings probably result from the heavy influence the highly-jeweled Biscuit and Robo, the Kids' bodyguards, have had on him.) Joe usually just wears a plain button-down shirt or T-shirt with Levi's 501 jeans — but spices things up with a Mickey Mouse or Felix The Cat jacket. (He just loves cartoon characters.) Joe changed his hairstyle last winter — instead of letting Reynaldo blow out his short sandy brown hair to the usual straight style, he decided to go with his natural curls. (A lot of people thought Joe permed his hair, but his hairdresser says the curls are natural.) Now he looks cherubic — and more adorable than ever, if that's possible!

NKOTB Dance Fever —
Catch It!

Everyone knows that the New Kids are about dancing as much as they're about singing. These guys started out on the streets of Boston perfecting their dance steps, and can invent new ones on a moment's notice. During a particularly good night onstage in concert, it's not unusual for the guys to do some impromptu shuffling in between the choreographed dance steps for each song. Following is an analysis of the Kids' dance steps one by one. Each has his own style, ranging from traditional to modern, and when they come together onstage, the chemistry is magnetic!

Danny

Danny's dancing is totally ahh-some — both the fans and music biz professionals consider him the best dancer in the group. Danny's extremely flexible and has perfected all his dance skills from break-dancing (which he used to do on a broken-up cardboard box on the streets of his neighborhood) to the traditional "soul dancing" of the great R&B groups of the '60s.

During Danny's solo spot in a New Kids concert, which comes about three-quarters of the way into the show, you can see five to ten minutes of the break-dancing routine that made him famous on the streets of Boston — and when he's feeling particularly limber, he'll spin on his head. (Please, do not attempt to do this, Blockheads)!

Jordan

Jordan has a more traditional dance style than Danny. He does such romantic dances that the girls in the front row often pass out, but just as he's gliding along like Fred Astaire, he'll throw in an Elvis Presley wiggle and tradition goes out the window! To relax before a show, Jordan tapdances in a dark corridor of the arena — but he has never gotten around to getting a pair of real tap shoes!

Joe

Joe has starred in local theater productions, including versions of *Oliver* and *Our Town*, since he was in

the sixth grade and so brings a chorus line tradition of dancing to the New Kids. When Joe joined the group in early '85, Maurice Starr had him study videotapes of the young Michael Jackson and Jackson's influence on Joe's dancing is apparent. Joe admits that since he's the youngest and smallest, he has a hard time keeping up with the other Kids — but fans think he's doing just fine!

Jon

Being the leggiest member of the New Kids — and having a runner's physique — helps Jon Knight lead the way during some of the New Kids' tougher dance

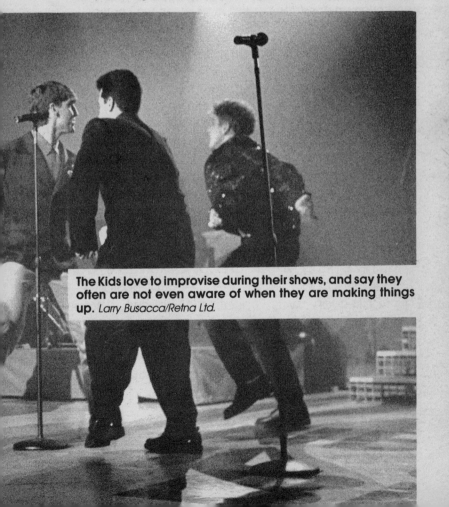

The Kids love to improvise during their shows, and say they often are not even aware of when they are making things up. *Larry Busacca/Retna Ltd.*

The Kids can invent new dance steps on a moment's notice, and often demonstrate this skill in between the choreographed steps for each song. *Ebet Roberts*

routines. Jon loves dancing in unison like the great soul groups of the '60s and is a real killer at doing those dizzying spins. Jon takes his dancing a step further when he runs out onto the catwalk set up during his segment of NKOTB performances — he kind of "dance-runs" as he sings his numbers.

Donnie

What can be said about Donnie Wahlberg except that he's a wild man onstage and literally serves as the "ringmaster" of the group. During one part of the performance he even wears a circus ringmaster's sequined, long-tailed tuxedo jacket! Like Danny, Donnie also danced on the streets of Boston — but his obsession was imitating Michael Jackson's "moonwalk." While Donnie does borrow a few steps from Michael Jackson, some fans will argue that he dances more like Tom Jones when he takes off his shirt, throws it to the ground, and then shimmies and shakes. Let's just say that Donnie has a lot of flash and that the steps he invents make a lot of fans' boyfriends jealous!

28

Those Quotable Kids

Joe
On Performing
"We will keep making stuff up. Like, this show might be different from tomorrow's show. You know, we just improvise more and more as the show goes on. We try out different stuff. You might be making up an idea and not even know about it!"

On The Road
"We get exhausted, but it's a pleasant type of exhaustion. You're kind of running on 'e,' but you get rejuvenated when you get onstage again — or get recognized. There's a price you gotta pay to do this — and that's really pushing yourself beyond your energy level and giving up a lot of personal time."

On His College Plans
"When I go to college, I want to be really serious about it and not be doing anything else. I will delay going, though, if the New Kids are still going strong. I just believe in giving 100 percent to what you're doing. I don't do anything halfway."

Danny
On The Road
"Our routine on the road is pretty consistent. We have soundchecks at 4:00 p.m. and things usually go pretty smoothly. The rest of the day we're either doing interviews or photo sessions or recording or a zillion other things. The work never stops, but we don't mind."

On His Future
"I just want to stick with the New Kids — wherever

that may take me. But if it (the group) ends, I might take up the scholarship that was offered to me from Boston University and major in engineering. I want this to never end, though. I hope we're always together."

On The Funniest Thing A Fan Ever Did

"One fan made a doll that looks like me — which is funny since we have our real dolls (from Hasbro) coming out in August."

Donnie

On Acting Happy All The Time

"Oh, I've *always* been like this. Performing makes me happy, whether it's for 50,000 people . . . or five! I think I was born to be on a stage. No joke. It ain't no lie!"

On Friendships Within The Band

"We're all good friends. That's the total truth. I think things wouldn't have worked out this well if we weren't so close!"

On A Great Vacation Day

"I just like to kick back for a while. It's something I hardly ever get to do anymore. It's so nice to be back home in my old bed. I can't tell you what it feels like. And I also like to kick back at the kitchen table with some takeout Northside burgers and a large container of milk. That sounds silly, but sometimes you miss the simple pleasures in life. But I have no complaints about being in the New Kids and totally dedicating myself to them. Things are getting better by the minute, and I'm certainly glad about that!"

Jordan

On His Relationship With Jon

"Sometimes we get in each other's hair — but we've really learned a lot about each other by tour-

For Danny, it's a "live and let live" type of girl; for Donnie, one who is assertive, smart and funny; Joe is looking for someone with plain and simple tastes; Jordan wants a fun-loving, life-of-the-party type, while Jon's girl will have to have her own hobbies and lead her own life. *Ebet Roberts*

ing together. But I have to admit one thing — when we finally get to go home, I don't care if I don't look at Jonathan's face for a week! I guess I'd rather spend time with the rest of my family while on break since I don't get to see a whole heck of a lot of them."

On The Fans

"I wish them all the luck in the world because they are the people who make the New Kids successful — not anyone else. We love the sound of their screams. We hear those screams in our dreams at night — it's not scary, it's nice."

On The New Kids' Disagreements With Each Other

"We don't have serious fights . . . *ever*, though we've had some tiffs over little things. Once, somebody was mad at somebody else because they borrowed a T-shirt and gave it back dirty . . . and it was like the guy's favorite T-shirt. But nothing more serious than that ever happens."

Jon
On The Fans

"Our fans are the best. Thanks for everything! You're the greatest — and we're not just saying that. We *mean* it!"

On His Relationship With Tiffany

"We have the same manager now, so of course the New Kids and Tiffany get linked up a lot. We've had our pictures taken with her at parties a lot and that encourages rumors. We're great friends, but there's never been anything romantic."

On The Newest Album, *Step By Step*

"There's a lot of stuff you can dance to, first of all. And second of all, we did more work on this album than on previous ones. We had a lot more input. Maurice advises us, but he lets us mess around in the studio more these days."

NKOTB's Proudest Moments . . . And Most Embarrassing!

Just like anyone else, superstars have moments they cherish and others they'd like to forget. The New Kids, fortunately, have a good sense of humor and can laugh off embarrassing situations.

Jordan Knight

Proudest Moment: "That has to be getting my platinum album for *Hangin' Tough*. A close second was playing the Boston Centrum last New Year's Eve. All our family members were there and we all were bursting with pride. It was a show that sold out in two or three hours."

Most Embarrassing Moment: "I've had a lot of embarrassing moments. One girl's boyfriend started chasing me around outside by the tour bus one night, but our bodyguards came to the rescue. This guy thought that I was going out with his girlfriend even though I never even met the girl! Also, there have been times when the other guys got flowers sent backstage and I didn't get any. I felt like a loser, but I guess I'm more the type you give teddy bears to!"

Donnie Wahlberg

Proudest Moment: "When Mary Alford (formerly Maurice Starr's assistant) gave me a copy of our first album. I was so thrilled I almost cried. We had worked so hard to get to that point."

Most Embarrassing Moment: "I have a lot of those. I don't realize the goofy faces I make for pictures,

33

and when I finally see them really printed in magazines, I'm really embarrassed and want to buy all the magazines off the newsstand! A really embarrassing moment I had in front of the Sweet Sensation girls came when I was driving a little golfcart around backstage — and they watched me crash right into a wall. Fortunately, I wasn't hurt, but in interviews they still talk about how bad a driver I am!"

Joe McIntyre

Proudest Moment: "Getting platinum records . . . and being able to have enough money to buy my mom a mink coat. She's deserved one for years. She's always been really supportive of me because she was an actress in local musical theater years ago."

Most Embarrassing Moment: "Probably having my pants split open a couple of years ago when we were opening for Tiffany. Tiff was watching us from the wings and she started cracking up. Another embarrassing moment came at the end of our tour with Sweet Sensation. The girls kept throwing stuffed animals up onstage at us and some hit me straight in the head and I couldn't keep up with the other guys. Yeah, that's another thing — sometimes I have trouble keeping up with the other guys onstage — they have longer legs than me, so they move faster. It's not fair!"

Jon Knight

Proudest Moment: "When we first started headlining at arenas, and I knew we had made it. I'm also really proud when I hear our songs on the radio."

Most Embarrassing Moment: "Getting announced on a TV show as *Jordan Knight!* Also, once this deejay in the Midwest who was introducing us in concert said, 'Here they are . . . Nude Kids On The Block!' I was blushing like crazy!"

Danny Wood

Proudest Moment: "Getting to do some engineering on *Hangin' Tough* and I am also very proud about how many copies the record sold. It proves those people wrong who say we are 'lightweight pop.'"

Most Embarrassing Moment: "The guy who screens our calls from our 900 hotline number told me that I get the weirdest. Why me? Let's see, what else has happened that's embarrassing? I guess having my pants rip onstage — that's why I always wear baggy ones now and play it safe."

Jordan's proudest moment was getting his platinum album for *Hangin' Tough*. *Steve Granitz/Retna Ltd.*

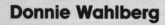

T-Rific Trivia Section

Donnie Wahlberg

• Donnie is the thinker of the group and a voracious reader. His favorite book is *The Autobiography Of Malcolm X,* which he believes should be mandatory reading for all freshmen in high school.

• Donnie's brother has a group called Marky Mark and The Funky Bunch; they'll be managed by Dick Scott once they cinch a record deal. (They just recorded their demo tapes in March.)

• Donnie stands 5'11", while his mom, Alma, is a diminutive 5'2".

• Donnie's favorite topic of conversation (outside of music) is world peace. He has embraced the peace symbol of the '60s very closely, and has them on much of his wardrobe. His favorite expression is "Peace out!"

• Donnie worships Paula Abdul and calls her "the prettiest lady in the world." (Needless to say, he looks forward to the day he'll get to meet her.)

• Donnie has said that he prefers women in the 25 to 30 age range. (That's 'cause he likes how mature-acting they are!)

• Donnie's favorite drink is water.

• Donnie says that the best burgers in the world are from the northside of Boston, not too far from where the Northside Boys, the group he produces, live.

• Donnie loves ripped up jeans. When they get a little too ripped up, a representative from Dick Scott Entertainment coaxes them away from him. (They're usually given away in a contest!)

• Donnie was inspired to go into show business because of Michael Jackson's mega-success, and he used to imitate Jackson at school and during family gatherings.

● Donnie loves the Muppets, and his favorite character is Cookie Monster.

Donnie devotes a lot of time to helping new groups such as The Northside Boys (old friends of his), and Marky Mark and the Funky Bunch (his brother's group). *Steve Granitz/Retna Ltd.*

Jon Knight

● Jon has to eat extra food when he's on the road, as he loses weight easily while traveling. (He hates how thin his face looks when he loses weight!)

● Jon got Jordan to join the church choir.

● Jon's mom says that he doesn't leave on tour without giving her a big bear hug!

● Jon's fondest memories of his childhood are going to his maternal grandmother's house in Ontario during summer vacation.

● Jon prefers to be called by his full name, Jonathan. (Sorry!)

- Jon's favorite stage outfit is the one he wears at the beginning of a NKOTB concert that looks like a toy soldier's outfit. (You know, that red jacket with the padded shoulders and big gold buttons that he wears with straight black jeans.)
- Jon loves the syndicated TV show, *This Old House*, which demonstrates various household handicrafts — such as building hammocks and making bookshelves. "I like to make things out of wood and watching *This Old House* helps me learn how to do it," he says. (Jordan chuckles, "Yeah, he's got that show on all the time!")
- Jon believes his biggest flaw is his "weak" chin.
- Jon loves to play Nintendo video games.
- Jon likes independent girls who understand his demanding schedule as a rock 'n' roller.
- Jon loves rugby shirts!
- Jon thinks he looks better in serious photos than ones in which he's smiling! (He's not giving that beautiful smile of his enough credit.)
- Jon's still wondering why his Shar-Pei, Houston, is always called "Nikko" in the press!

Joe McIntyre

- Joe has seven sisters and a brother — and he's the youngest. (His oldest sibling, Judy, is 18 years older than he is!)
- Joe has a penchant for Mickey Mouse and Felix The Cat memorabilia!
- Joe misses his mom's meatloaf when he's on the road!
- Joe believes his eyes are his worst feature, though everyone else thinks that they are his *best* feature.
- Joe loves his rare day off more than just about anything.

- Joe's voice changed right after recording "Please Don't Go Girl," so now when he sings it in concert, he's got to sing it in a lower key!

- Joe sings a Jackson Five cover song during every concert. Not surprisingly, he began loving the J-5 right after Maurice Starr gifted him with the three-record set, *Jackson Five Anthology*, upon joining the New Kids in April 1985.

- Joe says his biggest onstage asset is his singing ability, while his worst is his dancing. (He admits to having slight problems during dance numbers where the Kids dance in unison!)

- Joe's first favorite singer was Elton John and his current fave is Frank Sinatra.

- Joe believes that the key to the New Kids' success is that they are just like their fans!

- Joe loves to make his own ice cream sundaes — something that's not easily done on the road.

- Joe thinks that being the youngest member of a big family "is the greatest thing in the world. I was really pampered — but I don't think I was spoiled. There *is* a difference!"

- Joe just completed his senior year at a Catholic high school in his native Jamaica Plains, MA, and managed to remain an honor student even though he was out on the road most of the time!

- Joe's mom and dad had to move out of their house a few months back when the fans standing outside all the time got to be a little much!

- Joe's sister Judy is writing a screenplay about the boys.

- Right now, Joe is worried about his high school graduation ceremony — he really wants to attend, but is afraid the fans might get out of hand.

- What's the strangest thing that ever happened to Joe in relation to his fans? He explains, "One day I was at a pizza place and I left a crust on my plate. The minute I was walking out the door a girl grabbed it. I guess she wanted a souvenir. I can't get over stuff like that."

- Joe tries his best not to discuss NKOTB when he is home — he says that while he's with the family and friends, he just wants to lead a "regular" life.

Jordan Knight

- Jordan gets embarrassed when fans refer to him as the "cute one" of the group.
- Jordan loves nothing more than to hang out at Boston's Hi Fi pizza store — that's where the guys have hung out since even before they had a recording deal!
- Jordan says his biggest faults are that he can be very blunt — and that he bites his nails!
- Jordan thinks he has ugly feet, which he hides in the sand when he goes to the beach!
- Jordan is always chewing gum — at least until he walks out onstage.
- Jordan's two middle names are Nathaniel and Marcel.
- The first song Jordan ever learned was "With You All The Way" by New Edition.
- Jordan still doesn't believe he is cute!
- Jordan loves to snack after concerts — he loves chocolate, especially candy bars and shakes!
- Jordan says his best vocal work was done on "I'll Be Loving You (Forever)."
- Jordan loves to be out in the sun. (He just has to make sure that none of his tan lines are revealed when he takes his shirt off in concert!)
- Jordan's mom calls him her "enchanted one."
- In kindergarten, Jordan portrayed Baby Jesus in a school play.

40

- Jordan likes outgoing girls who laugh a lot!
- Jordan claims that he has never dated anyone steadily — but hopes to find that special girl sometime in the future!
- Jordan has two Siamese cats, Buster and Missy.
- Jordan hates when people tell him to cut off his braid. (To be honest, his mom isn't too crazy about it!)
- Jordan blushes when people tell him he looks like a young Elvis Presley!
- Jordan dressed up as Santa Claus every night during the New Kids' Winter '89 concert tour.
- Jordan is determined to learn how to ride a unicycle, and now can ride one without training wheels!
- Jordan's biggest energy pick-me-up on the road is sipping orange juice!
- Jordan's biggest mistake in a TV interview was saying that fans go to his family's home and take bags of grass, prompting even *more* fans to go to the Knight home and do the same.

Danny Wood

- Danny is often told that he looks like John Travolta!
- Danny is considered the best dancer of the group.
- Danny is an old schoolmate of Donnie's and was the second guy to join the New Kids.
- Danny is a novice recording engineer.
- Danny does some wonderful graffiti-style paintings.
- The other guys rub their heads up against Danny's before each show, hoping that his energy will rub off on them!
- Danny made up his mind to get off the streets one night after he saw a violent argument in front of a Boston nightspot.
- Danny has the lowest voice in the group and sings baritone.

- Danny, a serious weightlifter, can lift a 240-pound barbell even though he weighs just 162 pounds!
- Danny's gained 14 pounds since November — and it's all sheer muscle.
- Danny wears a gold hoop in his left ear.
- Danny had a steady girlfriend last year, but they have broken up due to the pressures of the road.
- Danny's mom says he's got a smile like Howdy Doody!
- Danny has a curly ponytail that at first his mother didn't approve of.
- Danny and his family live in a 10-room blue Victorian house in Boston.
- Danny is named after his dad.
- Danny is a mixture of Portuguese and Irish! (And it's quite a stunning mixture at that!)
- Danny played Mrs. Claus to Jordan's Santa Claus during the New Kids' Winter '89 shows — and even sported a long blond wig and a white terrycloth robe!
- Danny is 5'7½".
- Danny is one of six kids.
- Danny loves to walk around Boston's Charles River at night and see his favorite town all lit up. His favorite date is having dinner at a quiet Italian or Chinese restaurant and then going for a walk along the river.
- Danny's nickname is "Puff McCloud" — it's a fake detective name, and the Kids call him that because he always wants to get to the bottom of things (whether it's a problem at soundcheck or in his personal life!).

Guide To The
New Kids' Opening Acts

The Kids haven't forgotten the days when they were a new and struggling act, and so they try to lend a helping hand to some of their favorite up-and-comers. Following is a list of performers who have opened for the boys — and they all hold a dear place in the Kids' hearts. (The Kids sincerely hope they helped these acts get their "break"!)

Tiffany

After opening for Tiffany in Summer '88, things took off for the Kids and Tiffany got the opening slot on *their* tour. Although Tiff is lying low right now, she *did* introduce the New Kids during their March 15th, 1990, pay-per-view concert at New York's Nassau Coliseum — and with new manager Dick Scott as her guide, she'll have another hit record in no time!

Dino

This 26-year-old former Las Vegas deejay is a singer/songwriter whom Joe McIntyre thinks the world of. Dino's current album *24/7*, is at the top of the dance music charts, and he'll be releasing a new disc this summer. He toured with the New Kids throughout Winter '89.

Sweet Sensation

These three pretty ladies who all reside in Queens, NY, went to the top of the charts last fall with their megahit "Sincerely Yours," and their debut LP *Take It While It's Hot.* Follow-up album *Love Child* is a big hit. Simply going under their first names — Margie, Sheila and Betty — these gals are the hottest act

43

on the Latin and dance scenes today. They toured with the New Kids all through Winter '89, but in January went back to New York to record their new album for Atco Records.

Twenty-year-old Tommy Page who has a hit single, "I Will Be Your Everything," will accompany the New Kids on their "Magic Summer" tour. *Robin Platzer*

Cover Girls

This hot Capitol Records act toured with the New Kids in February and March. Consisting of Queens' natives Louise "Angel" Sabater, Caroline Jackson Calister and Margo Urban, these girls just can't go wrong. (Interestingly enough, their debut LP and hit single is "We Can't Go Wrong"!)

Perfect Gentlemen

This trio of youngsters from Boston includes Maurice Starr, Jr., 12, Corey Blakely, 11 (Maurice's next-door-neighbor) and Tyrone Sutton, 13 (who Maurice Starr,

Sr., discovered performing at local Roxbury rap shows). Their debut single and LP, "Ooh La La," is making fans say just that. (You might've caught their TV debut on *Showtime At The Apollo* last April.) The Gentlemen will be on tour with the New Kids throughout their "Magic Summer."

Tommy Page

This lucky 20-year-old is originally from West Caldwell, New Jersey, but now resides in Los Angeles. He is currently riding high on the charts with the hit single, "I Will Be Your Everything," for which he shares vocal, production and writing credits with The Crickets (you know who they are). Tommy's current album is called *Paintings In My Mind* and he will be on tour with the Kids for their entire "Magic Summer" tour.

Northside Boys

Donnie's friends from the Northside of Boston still haven't signed a record deal, but should be "inked" with a major label by the end of the summer. They opened a few shows for the Kids last winter, and their rap/pop sound went over in a big way. Donnie can't wait to get into the studio to help them record their debut disc and says he wants nothing more in the world than to see them go "over the top."

Bobby Ross Avila

This 13-year-old "music man" from San Bernadino, California is presently riding high with his RCA debut LP named — *what else*?! — *Music Man*! Following in the footsteps of his multi-talented father, Bobby Ross Avila, Sr., Bobby did just about everything on his debut disc, including playing several instruments, producing and songwriting. Bobby opened for the Kids in early '90, and will be having his own 900-hotline number from Info-Tainment, Inc., very soon!

Party Hearty — Hot Party Picks!

The New Kids have got to be one of the most fêted groups in the history of pop. But not only do they make appearances at their own bashes, but at fellow pop stars' as well. Here are a few highlights of the parties the boys thought were most memorable.

Tiffany's Birthday Party, September 1989 — This party, held at the popular Beverly Hills eatery Ed Debevic's (which has a 1950's theme) was a wonderful surprise for Tiff — for it was in honor of her 18th birthday. Lots of pix of Tiff and Jon Knight were taken, and when one was published in *People* magazine a few weeks later, rumors of a romance began flying!

Tiffany's *Other* Birthday Party, September 1989 — Yep, Tiff also got fêted by MCA Records at New York's Hard Rock Cafe. Many teen magazine editors and rock luminaries — especially Tiff's fellow MCA artists — showed up at the bash, which featured tons of finger food, including avocado sandwiches, ribs, petit fours and large bowls of guacamole with chips.

New Kids Christmas Party, Rockefeller Center, New York, November 1989 — To congratulate the guys on their sold-out shows at New York's Madison Square Garden, Columbia Records arranged for all three restaurants in Rockefeller Center to be closed for one night and invited press and celebrities to hang out with the Kids. Celebs in attendance included Salt 'N Pepa, The Cover Girls (who subsequently opened for the boys on tour), Def Duo (who is managed by Kids' road manager Peter Work) and Maurice Starr. Of course, all the moms and several family members were in attendance at this bash —

as 3,000 fans waited patiently outside by the famous Rockefeller Center rink all night.

Hal Jackson Tribute At The Apollo Theatre, New York, December 1989 — The Apollo Theatre is a home-away-from-home for many R&B acts, many of which are friends with the New Kids. The boys joined such rappin' buddies as Kid 'N' Play to help salute the legendary black deejay Hal Jackson during this particular night at the Apollo. The boys just love this legendary theatre, and try to hang out there when they're in New York — and people as diverse as Bill Cosby and Run-D.M.C. also call it their "home."

New Kids Press Party, Atlanta, January 1990 — Held at the Omni, the arena the guys were playing at, the boys were given a press bash by their management. All sorts of American and European teen press showed up to have one-on-one interviews with the boys, but unfortunately, Donnie and Jordan couldn't show because they were busy recording vocal tracks for the new *Step By Step* album.

New Kids Press Party, New Orleans, February 1990 — Held at the University of New Orleans Auditorium, the occasion was for the teen press to meet Angie Dirksen, 13, of Rock Valley, Iowa, winner of the "New Kids On The Block Talking Telephone Bulletin Board Contest." Angie and her parents and brother were flown to New Orleans for three days, attended the concert, and were invited backstage to meet the Kids (Angie also had her picture taken with Joe and Jon). And — as if that weren't exciting enough — Angie and her family were then treated to a four-day stay at Disneyworld!

New Kids
Hall Of Fame Awards

Everything about the New Kids is special — but some things are a bit more special than others. Here are our (and fans') favorite things about the New Kids — and in honor of these favorite things, we're presenting the New Kids Hall Of Fame Awards!

Best Eyes

No doubt about it, this award goes to **Joe** for having the most innocent, baby blue eyes in the world. Just one look at those eyes and you know how sweet 'n' sincere he is.

Best Lips

Awarded to **Jordan** for his cherry-red lips. This cutie has matinee-idol type looks and his mouth really says it all — if you'll pardon the pun!

Best Nose

Joe gets another one — that button nose is a real cutie and is perfect for his small face!

Best Hair

Let's give this one to **Danny** — that luxurious thick black hair is a real traffic-stopper, and the ponytail in back adds just the right touch of hipness.

Best Cheekbones

Jon's high cheekbones win hands down!

Best Complexion

This one goes to **Jon** as well — there's never a pimple to be found on his peaches 'n' cream complexion!

Best Physique

A tie between **Danny** and **Donnie.** They both put their time in at the gym. Danny has the most muscular arms while Donnie has the most muscular legs.

Donnie says "As long as we're in demand we'll be out there! We love to give the fans things to look forward to."
Larry Busacca/Retna Ltd.

Best Fashion Sense

This award goes to **Jon** — they don't call him "GQ" for nothing.

Best Voice

This award goes to **Jordan** for his smooth 'n' soulful

tenor — and for taking lead on the songs that are most difficult to sing.

Best Dancer

Danny has all the "right stuff" in this department. (See the NKOTB Dance Fever chapter for more info on his winning form!)

Most Friendly

Joe probably gets this award because he's always the first guy out of the dressing room to meet fans backstage after a show.

Smartest Kid

This one's a tie between **Joe** and **Danny** — while Joe has been on the honor role at Catholic Memorial High in Jamaica Plains, Massachusetts for four years, Danny *did* get a full scholarship to Boston University!

Most Outgoing

This award goes to **Donnie** for always going out of his way to make people — whether they be fans or interviewers — feel comfortable. He learned his great social skills from being in a big family and learning how to share everything!

Most Polite

While all the guys are super gentlemen, **Jon** is the most well-mannered — the one who reminds the others to "keep your elbows off the table."

Most Valuable Player

This award goes to **Donnie.** He not only sings and dances, but he plays drums and writes songs with Maurice Starr. He also has a lot of other "irons in the fire" — including producing his old buddies The Northside Boys and his brother's group, Marky Mark and The Funky Bunch.

Making Magic —
Summer '90 And Beyond!

The Kids have a lot of irons in the fire. April '90 saw the Kids go on a major European tour, and then come back to the States for a tour to coincide with the release of their fourth LP, *Step By Step*. The summer tour — which features openers Tommy Page and The Perfect Gentlemen — will be sponsored by Coca-Cola and be called the "Magic Summer Concert Tour." Why is Coca-Cola sponsoring the tour? Because the Kids will be doing up to five commercials for the famed beverage maker. The first commercial was taped at the beginning of April at a soundstage in LA, and the first one aired on Memorial Day weekend!

According to Michael A. Beindorff, Vice-President, Marketing Planning, Coca-Cola USA, "New Kids On The Block capture the spirit and imagination of consumers of Coca-Cola everywhere. They will help provide an unsurpassed summer of fun." The Kids inked their precedent-setting promotional pact for Coca-Cola Classic March 3, during ceremonies at the Coca-Cola Company headquarters in Atlanta, Georgia. Later that evening, the group performed for a sold-out audience at Atlanta's Omni Arena.

The summer will also mark another great achievement for the band. In August, Hasbro Toys will introduce a line of lifelike New Kids dolls. Fans will not only be able to buy these adorable 11¼" high dolls, but outrageous stage clothes, too. There's even a stage set, complete with a stage, microphone and amplifiers. No doubt that once these hot products hit the toy store shelves, everyone will be stocking up on them for Christmas gifts.

The guys will take a couple weeks off this summer to do the voices for their upcoming self-titled ABC Saturday morning cartoon, and then in October and November, do their long-awaited feature film and Christmas special. The guys say their next album will be the soundtrack to their movie, which should be out in late winter/early spring 1991.

As Donnie so aptly puts it, "As long as we're in demand we'll be out there! We love to give fans things to look forward to."

Danny, Jordan, Joe, Donnie, and Jon (left to right) opening Coca-Cola "MagiCans." The Kids will appear in five new TV commercials for "Magic Summer 90" and in June will launch their new "Magic Summer" concert tour. *Courtesy of Coca-Cola*

Just The Facts, Ma'am!

Donnie Wahlberg
Full Name: Donald Edmund Wahlberg, Jr.
Nicknames: Donnie, Cheese
Birthdate: August 17, 1969
Birth Sign: Leo
Home: Dorchester, Massachusetts
Weight: 155 lbs.
Height: 5'11"
Eye Color: Hazel
Hair: Blond
Parents: Alma and Donald
Siblings: Brothers Mark, Bobbo, Jimbo, Paul, Arthur and sisters Michelle, Debbie and Tracey
Fave Male Singers: Aaron Hall (from Guy), rapper Chuck D., Bobby Brown, and of course, Jordan Knight
Fave Food: "Depends on my mood. I always enjoy home cooking."
Fave Drink: Water
Fave Book: *Autobiography of Malcolm X*
Fave School Subject: "Math — it always has a solution."
Fave Sport: Baseball
Biggest Turn-On: Learning something new
Ambition: "To live to see the day when this country lives up to its reputation."
Message To Fans: "Try not to judge things 'til you've been educated on them."

Danny Wood
Full Name: Daniel William Wood, Jr.
Nickname: Puff McCloud
Birthdate: May 14, 1970

53

Birth Sign: Taurus
Home: Boston, Massachusetts
Weight: 162 lbs.
Height: 5'7½"
Eye Color: Brown
Hair: Black
Parents: Daniel and Elizabeth (Betty)
Siblings: Bethany, Melissa, Pam, Brett and Rachel
Fave Male Singers: Howard Hewitt, Peabo Bryson
Fave Female Singer: Patti LaBelle
Fave Music Group: Hall & Oates
Fave TV Show: *America's Most Wanted*
Snack Fave: Popcorn
Fave Book: *Slaughterhouse Five*
Fave New Kids Record: "This One's For The Children"
Fave Sport: Basketball
Hobbies: Relaxing, exercising
Biggest Turn-On: Kind and caring people
Biggest Turn-Off: A pushy know-it-all
Ambition: "To become a record producer."
Most Prized Possessions: Gold and platinum records

Joe McIntyre

Full Name: Joseph Mulrey McIntyre
Nicknames: Joey Joe, Bird, JoeBird
Birthdate: December 31, 1972
Birth Sign: Capricorn
Home: Jamaica Plains, Massachusetts
Weight: 130 lbs.
Height: 5'6"
Eye Color: Blue
Hair: Brown
Fave Car: Ford Mustang Convertible — 5.0
Parents: Katherine and Thomas
Siblings: Sisters Judy, Alice, Susan, Tricia, Carol, Jean and Kate and brother Tommy

Fave Male Singer: Frank Sinatra
Fave Female Singer: Anita Baker
Fave Movies: *Midnight Run, Godfather I & II*
Fave TV Show: *20/20*
Food Of Choice: Mom's meatloaf
Fave Snack: Lemonade & hot tamales
Fave Book: *Chocolate War*
Fave School Subject: U.S. History
Fave Sport: Golf
Fave Sports Team: Boston Celtics
Ambition: "To be a good person and to be happy."
Biggest Turn-On: "The excitement in the air before a show."
Biggest Turn-Off: "Being told you have a day off and then not having one."

Jon Knight

Full Name: Jonathan Rashleigh Knight
Birthdate: November 29, 1968
Birth Sign: Sagittarius
Home: Boston, Massachusetts
Weight: 155 lbs.
Height: 5'11"
Eye Color: Hazel
Hair: Brown
Parents: Marlene and Allan (Divorced)
Fave Car: Black BMW 535 or 735
Fave TV Show: "This Old House"
Fave Food: Italian or Mom's home cooking
Fave School Subject: Science
Fave Sports: Water sports including swimming, sailing and scuba diving
Hobbies: Shopping
Biggest Turn-On: Health, happiness and peace
Biggest Turn-Off: War, pollution, racism
Ambition: "To be as good as I can be in what I pursue."

Jordan Knight

Full Name: Jordan Nathaniel Marcel Knight
Nickname: "J"
Birthdate: May 17, 1970
Birth Sign: Taurus
Home: Dorchester, Massachusetts
Weight: 155-160 lbs.
Height: 5'11"
Eye Color: Brown
Hair: Brown
Parents: Marlene and Allan (Divorced)
Siblings: Sisters Allison and Sharon and brothers David, Chris and Jonathan
Fave Car: Porsche
Fave Male Singers: Luther Vandross, Michael Jackson, Stevie Wonder
Fave Flicks: *The Godfather, The Untouchables*
Fave Food: Bacon double deluxe burger with cheese
Fave Snacks: Twix bars, peanuts, gummy bears
Fave School Subjects: English, Social Issues, Music
Sports: Basketball, ping pong
Hobbies: Reading, watching movies
Biggest Turn-On: "People being nice to others."
Biggest Turn-Off: "People acting like jerks to each other because they're different."
Ambition: "To be happy in whatever I do."
Most Prized Possession: "My family."

Blockbusters

New Kids On The Block (Columbia, 1986)
Tracks: "Stop It Girl" (M. Starr); "Didn't I (Blow Your Mind)?" (W. Hart, T. Bell); "Popsicle" (M. Starr); "Angel" (M. Starr, J. Cappra); "Be My Girl" (M. Starr); "New Kids On The Block" (M. Starr, D. Wahlberg); "Are You Down?" (AJ, E. Nuri, K. Banks, D. Wahlberg); "I Wanna Be Loved By You" (M. Starr); "Don't Give Up On Me" (M. Starr); "Treat Me Right" (M. Starr).

Hangin' Tough (Columbia, 1988)
Tracks: "You Got It (The Right Stuff)" (M. Starr); "Please Don't Go Girl" (M. Starr); "I Need You" (M. Starr); "I'll Be Loving You (Forever)" (M. Starr); "Cover Girl" (M. Starr); "I Need You" (M. Starr); "Hangin' Tough" (M. Starr); "I Remember When" (M. Starr, E. Kelly, J. Randolph, C. Williams); "What'cha Gonna Do (About It)" (M. Starr); "My Favorite Girl" (M. Starr, D. Wahlberg, J. Knight); "Hold On" (M. Starr).

Merry, Merry Christmas (Columbia, 1989)
Tracks: "This One's For The Children" (M. Starr); "Last Night I Saw Santa Claus" (M. Starr, A. Lancellotti); "I'll Be Missin' You Come Christmas (A Letter To Santa)" (K. Nolan, M. Starr); "I Still Believe In Santa Claus" (M. Starr, A. Lancellotti); "Merry, Merry Christmas" (M. Starr, A. Lancellotti); "The Christmas Song (Chestnuts Roasting On An Open Fire)" (M. Torme, R. Wells); "Funky, Funky Xmas" (M. Starr, D. Wahlberg); "White Christmas" (I. Berlin); "Little Drummer Boy" (K.K. Davis, B. Onorati, H. Simeone, adaptation by J. Edwards); "This One's For The Children" (Reprise).

Step By Step (Columbia, 1990)
Tracks: Side One: "Step By Step" (M. Starr); "Tonight" (M. Starr, Al Lancelloti); "Baby, I Believe In You" (M. Starr); "Call It What You Want" (M. Starr); "Let's Try It Again" (M. Starr); "Happy Birthday" (M. Starr, M. Jonzun)

Side Two: "Games" (M. Starr, D. Wahlberg); "Time Is On Our Side" (M. Starr, A. Lancelloti); "Where Do We Go From Here?" (M. Starr); "Stay With Me, Baby" (M. Starr, M. Jonzun); "Funny Feeling" (M. Starr, M. Jonzun); "Never Gonna Fall In Love Again" (M. Starr, M. Jonzun, D. Wood)

Singles: Step By Step released 5/90; future singles not announced at press time.

Singles

"Be My Girl"
"Stop It Girl"
"Didn't I (Blow Your Mind)?"
"Please Don't Go Girl"
"You Got It (The Right Stuff)"
"I'll Be Loving You Forever"
"Cover Girl b/w Didn't I Blow Your Mind?"
"Hangin' Tough"
"This One's For The Children"
"Step By Step"

Videography

Music Videos

"Please Don't Go Girl"
"You Got It (The Right Stuff)"
"I'll Be Loving You Forever"
"Cover Girl"
"Didn't I (Blow Your Mind)?"
"Hangin' Tough"
"This One's For The Children"
"Step By Step"

Videocassettes

HANGIN' TOUGH (CBS Home Video, 1989)
This delightful 30-minute home video contains interviews and backstage footage guaranteed to delight any Blockhead! And let's not forget the videos for the four hits off the *Hangin' Tough* LP: "Please Don't Go Girl," "You Got It (The Right Stuff)," "I'll Be Loving You Forever" and "Hangin' Tough."

HANGIN' TOUGH LIVE (CBS Home Video, 1989)
Every New Kids hit off their dynamite second LP is performed live in this half-hour-long cassette. A must-have for die-hard collectors! There's nothing but straight music and dancin' on this fine home vid!

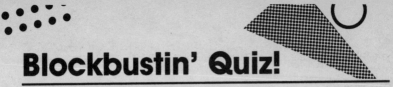

Blockbustin' Quiz!

The answers to the following 15 fill-in questions can be found in the text of this book. To see how you've done, check the answer key at the end of the quiz.

1. Which New Kid bought his mother a mink coat as a big thank you for all her support?

   _____

2. Which New Kid had experience in local Boston musical theater?

   _____

3. What New Kid's mom says he's got a smile like Howdy Doody?

   _____

4. What New Kid is producing the Northside Boys and Marky Mark and The Funky Bunch?

   _____

5. Which New Kid is nicknamed "GQ" by the other boys?

   _____

6. What is the name of the group featuring Maurice Starr, Jr.? (Hint: They're opening for NKOTB on their "Magic Summer" tour!)

   _____

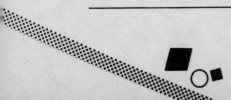

7. Which New Kid tapdances alone before going on stage in order to relax?

_____

8. Where did Columbia Records hold the recent Christmas bash they threw for NKOTB? (Hint: It's the site of a world-famous ice skating rink.)

_____

9. The New Kids have released two home videocassettes with similar titles. Name them.

_____ and _____

10. Who currently is Joe's favorite singer?

_____

11. Which two New Kids were born under the sign of Taurus?

_____ and _____

12. Which New Kid had a peace sign shaved into his head last year?

_____

13. Which Kid likes clothes featuring Mickey Mouse and Felix the Cat?

_____

14. Which New Kid had a very embarrassing moment backstage last year when he drove a golf cart into a wall with members of Sweet Sensation looking on?

15. This talented 20-year-old singer/songwriter's March '90 hit "I Will Be Your Everything" shared production, engineering and vocal credits with "The Crickets":

"We're all good friends . . . things wouldn't have worked out this well if we weren't so close," says Donnie, expressing the feelings shared by all the guys. *Robin Platzer*

Answer Key:
1. Joe   2. Joe   3. Danny   4. Donnie
5. Jon   6. Perfect Gentlemen   7. Jordan
8. Rockefeller Center   9. *Hangin' Tough; Hangin' Tough Live*   10. Frank Sinatra   11. Jordan; Danny   12. Donnie   13. Joe   14. Donnie
15. Tommy Page.

Danny, Donnie, Joe, Jordan, and Jon (left to right) all have high hopes for their newest album, *Step By Step*.
Larry Busacca/Retna Ltd.

How Did You Score?

Twelve to Fifteen Right!: Way Cool! You can rock around the block with these "Kids" anytime! You deserve to be president of their fan club.

Eight to Eleven Right: So, so! Maybe you'd better view your *Hangin' Tough* and *Hangin' Tough Live* video-cassettes a few more times and soak up the good vibes!

Below Eight Right: Oops, better go back and read this book again cover to cover.

TAKE THE
NEW
KIDS
ON THE
BLOCK
HOME WITH YOU!

You watch them, you read about them, you dream about them, you scream about them. And why not? They're the hottest guys on ANYONE'S block!

This fantastic, photo-filled, black and white scrapbook can be yours for ONLY $3.00 plus $1.00 for postage and handling per book.

SPECIAL FEATURE Spaces are provided so you can paste your own favorite pictures into this fabulous book!